THE LIFE CYCLE OF A

S N A K E

By Robin Merritt

Published by The Child's World®
1980 Lookout Drive
Mankato, MN 56003-1705
800-599-READ
www.childsworld.com

The Child's World®: Mary Berendes, Publishing Director
The Design Lab: Kathleen Petelinsek, design
Red Line Editorial: Editorial direction

ISBN: 978-1-60973-192-2
LCCN: 2011927743

Printed in the United States of America
Mankato, MN
July 2011
PA02089

TABLE OF

CONTENTS

LIFE CYCLES

Every living thing has a life cycle. A life cycle is the steps a living thing goes through as it grows and changes. Humans have a life cycle. Animals have a life cycle. Plants have a life cycle, too.

A cycle is something that happens over and over again. A life cycle begins with the start of a new life. It continues as a plant or creature grows. And it keeps going as one living thing creates another, or **reproduces**—and the cycle starts over again.

A snake's life cycle has three main steps: egg, snakelet, and adult snake.

The life cycles of plants and snakes are very different.

Many hard scales cover a snake's skin.

SNAKES

Like turtles and lizards, snakes are reptiles.
Reptiles are cold-blooded animals. This means
their body temperature changes with their
surroundings. That is why snakes bask, or lie,
in the sun to warm up. Or, they find a shady
area to cool off.

Snakes have scales on their skin. Some
people who have never touched a snake
expect them to feel slimy, like earthworms.
But their scales are hard like fingernails. They
make snakes feel dry and smooth.

Many ribs protect the long bodies of snakes. These ribs attach to many backbones. A person has 33 backbones, while a snake may have more than 200! They work like links in a chain to make its body extra flexible.

Clear scales cover and protect snake eyes like goggles. Snake eyes can see movement, but snakes cannot see far in front of them. Snake ears are not visible—they are inside their bodies. Snakes don't have strong hearing.

Smell is the most important sense for snakes. They flick out their tongues to pick up bits of scent. Inside their mouths, a special organ detects the smells of food and danger.

Snakes smell with their tongues.

Thin vine snakes are hard to see against green plants.

Snakes live on every continent except Antarctica. There are about 3,000 kinds of snakes. They can live on land, in trees, or in water. Only about 650 kinds have **venom** that is poisonous.

The smallest snake, the threadsnake, is only 4 inches (10 cm) long. But the largest snake, the anaconda, can grow as long as 38 feet (11.6 m). That's as long as a bus!

Snakes can be many colors. Some colors give snakes **camouflage**. They blend into their surroundings. Hidden, they can sneak up on **prey** or hide from **predators**. Other snakes have bright colors that warn away enemies.

OUT COME SNAKELETS

A snake's life starts inside an egg. It gets food from a yolk, just like a chick. In some snakes, the egg stays inside its mother's body for months as the baby snake grows. The shell softens, and the snakelet may wiggle free even before its mother pushes it out of her body.

Most snakes lay eggs on the ground or in a nest. A female python wraps herself around her eggs for more than two months to help keep them warm. But usually mother snakes leave their eggs alone with only the sun to warm them.

A python warms her clutch of eggs.

From its egg emerges a python snakelet.

Snake eggs feel like soft leather. When baby snakes are ready to hatch, they use an egg tooth on their snout to tear a slit in the shell. A snakelet wriggles out of the egg. It is on its own now. It slithers off in search of prey, such as slugs or caterpillars.

A NEW SUIT OF SCALES

As snakes grow bigger, their scaly skin doesn't stretch much. Young snakes will shed their skin, or **molt**, several times in their first year. Before molting, snakes crawl to safe places. The old skin splits near the mouth, and the snake rubs its body on rocks or branches until the skin slips off. Underneath is a new suit of scales.

Like fish, snakes grow throughout their lives. These reptiles grow fast for their first few years. Adult snakes also molt, but not as often. Their colors or patterns may change, too.

A snake slides out of its old skin when it molts.

Venom drips from the fangs of an attacking snake.

MEAT EATERS

Snakes are **carnivores**—they eat only meat. Some snakes hide under leaves and wait to strike. Others follow a scent trail. Young cantil snakes wiggle their yellow-tipped tails to look like worms. Lizards are fooled into coming closer, and the snakes attack.

Anacondas wrap their bodies around rats and squeeze. This snake is a **constrictor**. Other snakes bite their prey and swallow it live. A few kinds of snakes have long, sharp fangs. These teeth shoot venom into a prey's body. The venom kills or harms the animal so it is easier to eat.

Snakes swallow their prey whole, usually headfirst. Their jaws stretch wide open as they swallow animals many times larger than their mouth. Rock pythons can even swallow a gazelle!

After a snake swallows its prey, it rests while the food digests. Depending on the size of the meal, the snake may not have to eat again for months.

A viper snake widely opens its mouth to swallow a lizard.

A fox's prey is a small snake.

SNAKES ARE PREY, TOO

Other animals like to eat snakes, too. When enemies appear, snakes hide under rocks and leaves or hurry away. Rattlesnakes shake their tails to make a warning sound. The rattle cautions hungry coyotes to keep away. But many snakelets are still snatched up by frogs, birds, or bigger snakes. Adult snakes become meals for foxes, hawks, and other fierce predators. Snakes can survive up to 30 years, but few snakes in the wild live that long.

TOO HOT, TOO COLD

Because they are cold-blooded, snakes have to find ways of warming or cooling their bodies. Desert snakes often hunt at night to stay cool.

In places with cold winters, snakes must find a way to survive the chill. Usually, copperhead snakes live alone. But in late fall, they crawl into a rocky den with many other snakes. They curl up together to **hibernate**, or sleep deeply, through the winter. Their breathing and heartbeats slow down. When warm weather returns, the snakes wake up and crawl outside again.

A copperhead snake peeks out from its den.

Snakes gather in groups to mate.

THE LIFE CYCLE CONTINUES

Often in spring, snakes gather for a different reason. When snakes are three or four years old, they can reproduce. Male snakes may fight each other to win a female. Then the winning male and a female will mate. Eggs inside the female's body become fertilized. That means snakelets begin to grow inside. Some snakes have only one egg at a time, while others may have 100. The male snake goes to look for another mate, but the female looks for a safe place to lay her eggs.

A group of snake eggs is called a clutch. A clutch of corn snake eggs might remain under a log while the snakelets grow inside. If a raccoon digs them up, they will never hatch. But if the snakelets are lucky, in about two months they will hatch from their eggs. The snake life cycle will go on.

Baby corn snakes hatch from their eggs.

LIFE CYCLE DIAGRAM

Egg

Snakelet

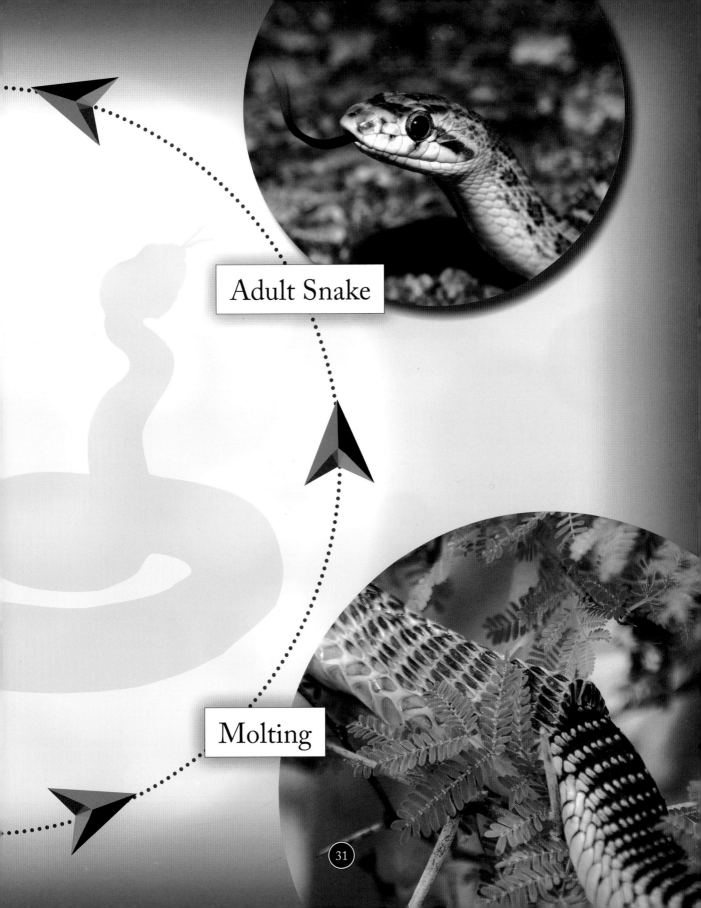

Adult Snake

Molting

Web Sites

Visit our Web site for links about the life cycle of a snake: **childsworld.com/links**

Note to Parents, Teachers, and Librarians: We routinely verify our Web links to make sure they are safe and active sites. So encourage your readers to check them out!

Books

Gibbons, Gail. *Snakes*. New York: Holiday House, 2007.
McDonald, Mary Ann. *Garter Snakes*. Chanhassen, MN: The Child's World, 2007.
Miller, Heather Lynn. *This Is Your Life Cycle*. New York: Clarion Books, 2008.

Glossary

camouflage (KAM-uh-flahzh): Camouflage is the coloring and markings that allow an animal to blend in with its surroundings. A vine snake's camouflage helps it look like plants.

carnivores (CAR-nuh-vorz): Carnivores are animals that eat other animals. Snakes are carnivores.

constrictor (kun-STRIKT-ur): A constrictor is a snake that wraps its body around an animal and squeezes it until it stops breathing. A python is a constrictor.

hibernate (HYE-bur-nate): To hibernate, an animal or insect spends the winter in a deep sleep, with slowed breathing and heartbeat. Many snakes often hibernate in one den.

molt (molt): To molt is to shed old skin and grow new skin. A snake will molt several times in its first year.

predators (PRED-uh-turs): Predators are animals that hunt and eat other animals. All snakes are predators.

prey (pray): Prey is an animal that is hunted by another for food. Hawks hunt snakes as their prey.

reproduces (ree-pruh-DOOS-ez): If an animal or plant reproduces, it produces offspring. A snake reproduces to make snakelets.

venom (VEN-um): Venom is a poison made by some snakes and is usually passed into an animal through a bite. A snake's venom can kill its prey.